At Sylvan, we believe that a lifelong love of learning begins at an early age, and we are glad you have chosen our resources to help your child experience the joy of mathematics to build critical reasoning skills. We know that the time you spend with your children reinforcing the lessons learned in school will contribute to their love of learning.

Success in math requires more than just memorizing basic facts and algorithms; it also requires children to make sense of size, shape, and numbers as they appear in the world. Children who can connect their understanding of math to the world around them will be ready for the challenges of mathematics as they advance to topics that are more complex.

At Sylvan we use a research-based, step-by-step process in teaching math that includes thought-provoking math problems and activities. As students increase their success as problem solvers, they become more confident. With increasing confidence, students build even more success. Our Page Per Day books are designed to help you to help your child build the skills and confidence that will contribute to success in school.

Included with your purchase of this Page Per Day book is a coupon for a discount at a participating Sylvan Learning center. We hope you will use this coupon to further your child's academic journey. To learn more about Sylvan and our innovative in-center programs, call 1-800-EDUCATE or visit www.SylvanLearning.com.

We look forward to partnering with you to support the development of a confident, well-prepared, independent learner.

The Sylvan Team

Tips for Math Success

Read books that contain numbers. Increase number awareness and recognition by reading books that feature numbers.

Play games with numbers. Let your child draw a hopscotch game on the sidewalk and then count out loud forward and backward.

Count everything. Encourage your child to count things in your home, outside, and at the store. Ask questions to foster your child's counting and to make it fun.

Use everyday items to reinforce concepts. Building block towers helps reinforce understanding of addition. Eating crackers is a good way for your child to understand subtraction. Be creative.

Don't forget measurement. Comparing amounts and sizes is part of math too. Compare heights of family members, the length of household items, or have your child measure big things using his or her feet.

Use pictures. Pictures of animals, pieces of pizza, or coin collections can help your child visualize and apply math concepts such as sorting by attributes.

Look for patterns. While setting the table for dinner use a repeating pattern of plates, glasses, and forks and have your child complete the pattern.

Pre-K Page Per Day:
Numbers

Published in the United States by Random House, Inc., New York, and in Canada by Random House of Canada Limited, Toronto.

www.tutoring.sylvanlearning.com

Producer & Editorial Direction: The Linguistic Edge
Writer: Kelly Woodard Parker
Cover and Interior Illustrations: Shawn Finley, Tim Goldman, and Duendes del Sur
Layout and Art Direction: SunDried Penguin

First Edition

ISBN: 978-0-307-94456-6
ISSN: 2161-993X

This book is available at special discounts for bulk purchases for sales promotions or premiums. For more information, write to Special Markets/Premium Sales, 1745 Broadway, MD 6-2, New York, New York 10019 or e-mail specialmarkets@randomhouse.com.

PRINTED IN THE USA

10 9 8 7 6 5 4 3

See It, Say It, Show It

This is the number 1. SEE the number. SAY the number. SHOW the number using your fingers. TRACE the 1 with your finger.

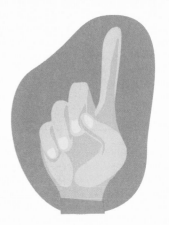

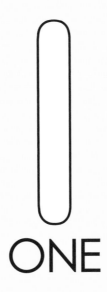

ONE

This is one wagon and one toy bear. DRAW one toy in the wagon.

Terrific Tracing

TRACE the number 1s. Start at the green arrow labeled with a number 1.

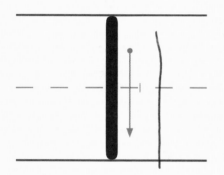

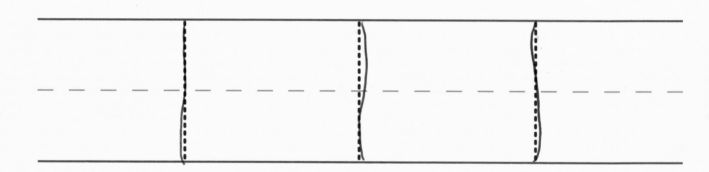

Now TRACE the number 1 next to each picture.

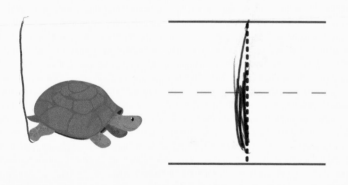

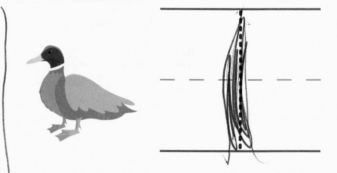

Which One?

CIRCLE the picture in each pair that shows **one**.

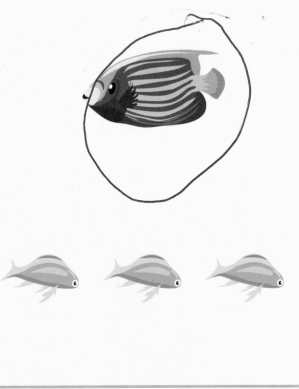

Hidden Picture

FIND the spaces that show either one picture or the number 1. COLOR those spaces red to see the hidden pictures.

See It, Say It, Show It

This is the number **2**. SEE the number. SAY the number. SHOW the number using your fingers. TRACE the **2** with your finger.

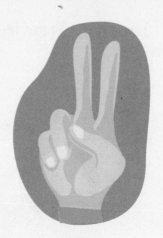

TWO

Here are two flowers. DRAW two vases.

Terrific Tracing

TRACE the number **2**s. Start at the green arrow labeled with a number 1.

Now TRACE the number **2** next to each picture.

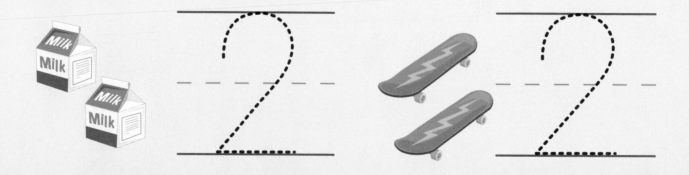

Cross Out

COLOR the number **2**. CROSS OUT the cards that do **not** show **two**.

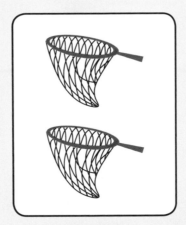

Match Up

TRACE the number **2**s. DRAW lines to match the **2**s with the correct pictures.

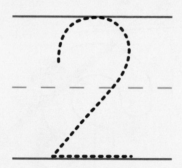

See It, Say It, Show It

This is the number **3**. SEE the number. SAY the number. SHOW the number using your fingers. TRACE the **3** with your finger.

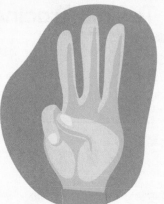

THREE

Here are three children and three balloons. DRAW three cupcakes on the plate.

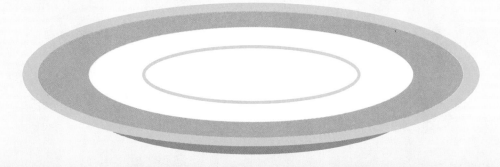

Terrific Tracing

TRACE the number **3**s. Start at the green arrow labeled with a number 1.

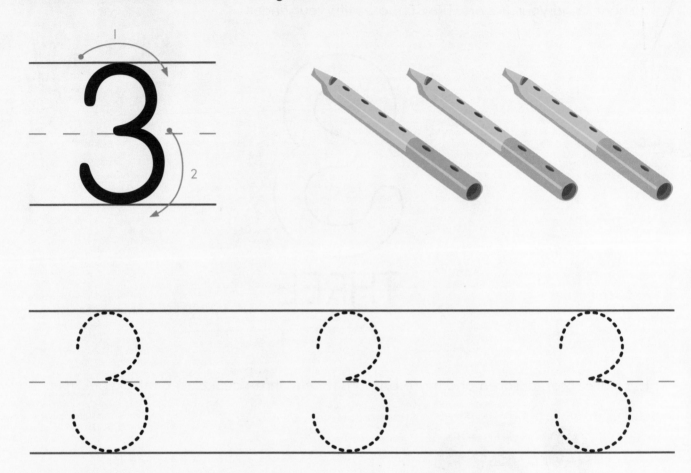

Now TRACE the number **3** next to each picture.

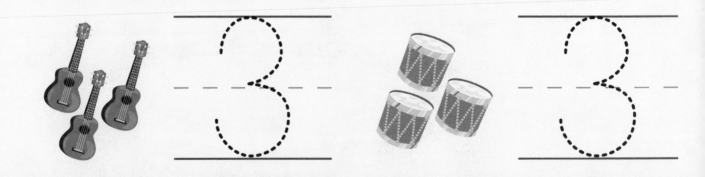

Hop to It

DRAW a line connecting the **3**s to help the frog hop safely across the pond.

START

3	1	2		2
3	3		1	
2	3	2		2
		3	1	
	2	3		

END

Number 3

Color It

SHOW the number **three** using your fingers. COLOR the three butterflies.

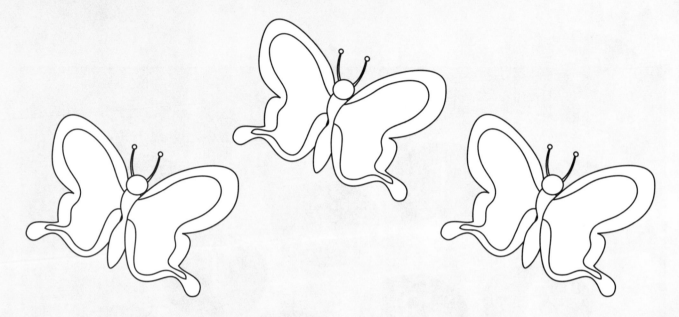

SHOW three fingers again. COLOR the three cakes.

See It, Say It, Show It

This is the number **4**. SEE the number. SAY the number. SHOW the number using your fingers. TRACE the **4** with your finger.

FOUR

Here is an ice cream cone with four scoops of ice cream. COLOR the four scoops.

Terrific Tracing

TRACE the number **4**s. Start at the green arrow labeled with a number I.

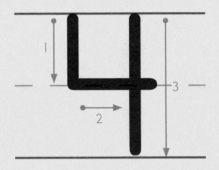

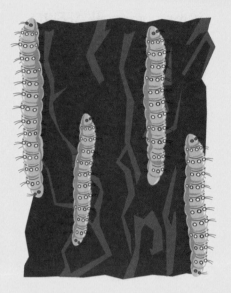

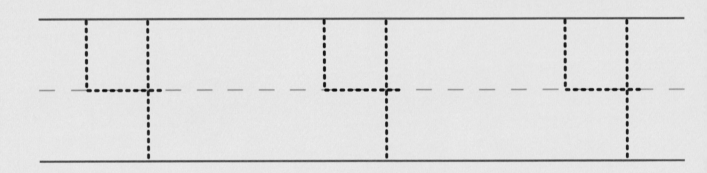

Now TRACE the number **4** next to each picture.

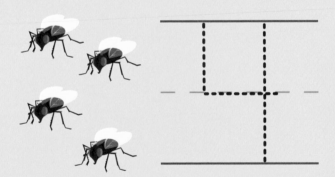

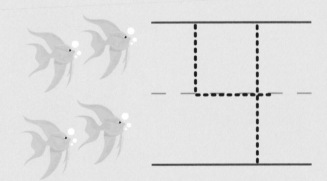

Can You Help?

LOOK at the map. FOLLOW the path marked with **4**s to help the postal carrier get to the mailbox.

Which One?

CIRCLE the picture in each pair that shows **four**.

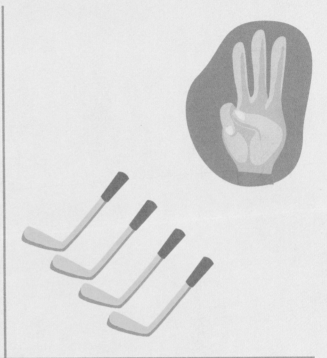

See It, Say It, Show It

This is the number **5**. SEE the number. SAY the number. SHOW the number using your fingers. TRACE the **5** with your finger.

FIVE

Here are five paint tubes. COLOR the tubes five different colors.

Terrific Tracing

TRACE the number **5**s. Start at the green arrow labeled with a number 1.

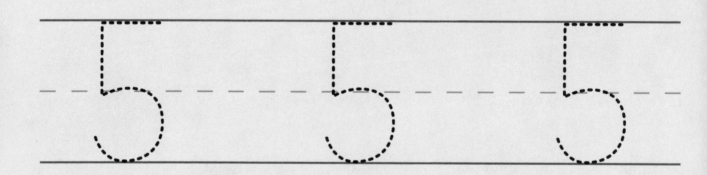

Now TRACE the number **5** next to each picture.

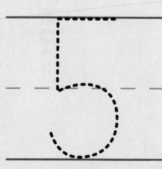

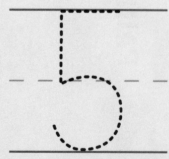

Put It Away

DRAW lines to put away the groups of five toys that belong in the toy box.

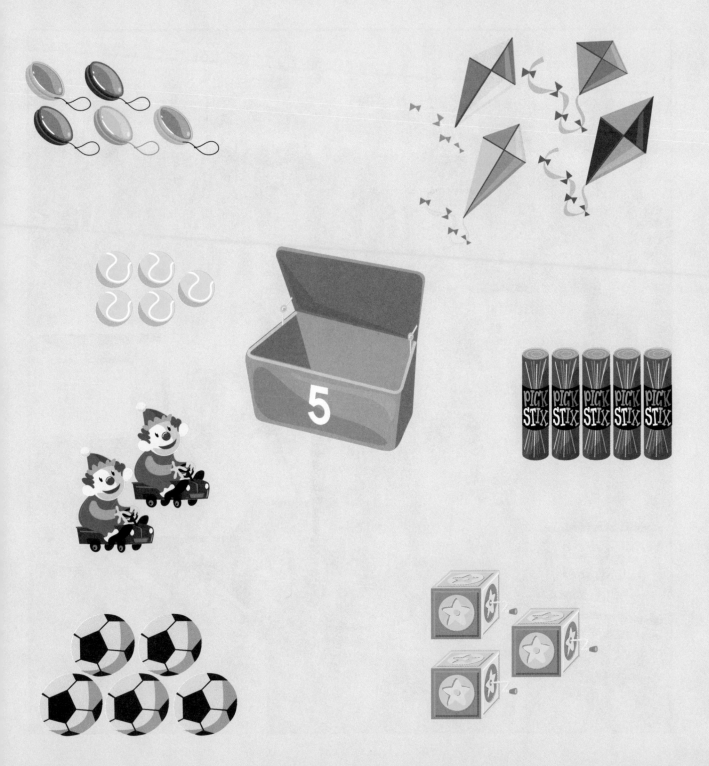

Hide and Seek

CIRCLE the 5s that are hiding in the picture.

More than Enough

LOOK at the toys. CIRCLE the child in each pair who has **more** toys.

Example:

Don't Mess with Less

LOOK at the fish bowls in each row. TRACE the number of fish in each bowl. CIRCLE the number that is **less** than the other number.

Example:

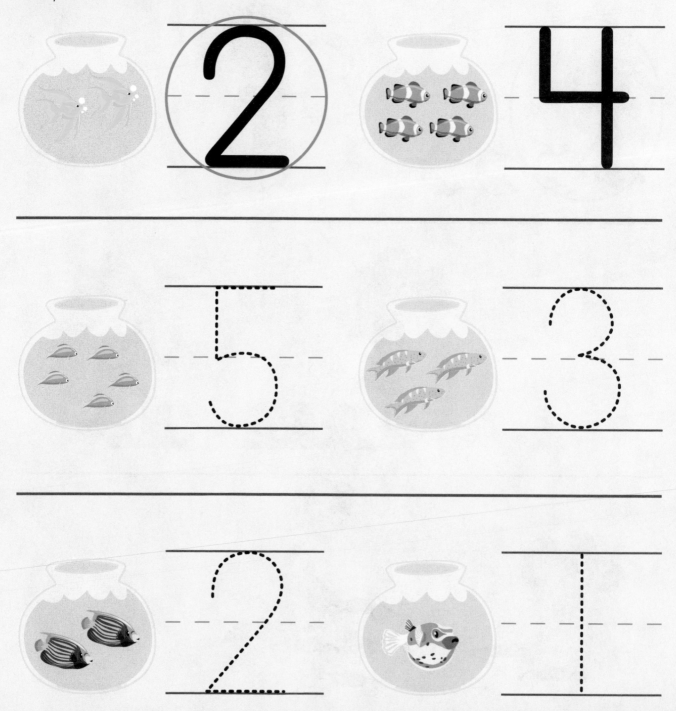

Circle the Same

COLOR the numbers. Then CIRCLE the pictures that match the number at the top.

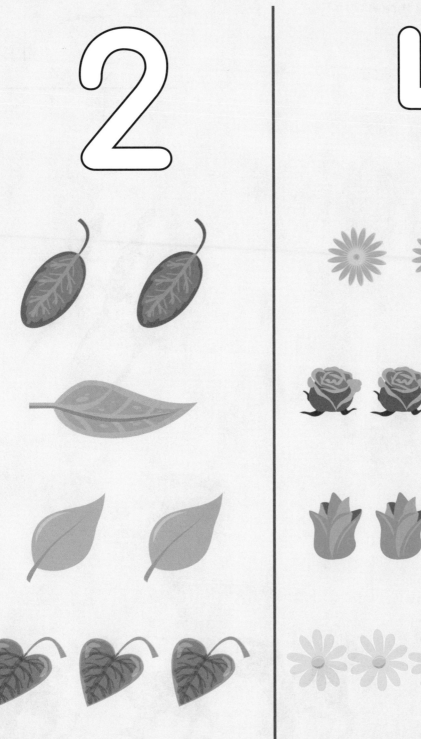

What's Different?

TRACE the number **3**. Then CROSS OUT the pictures that do **not** show **three**.

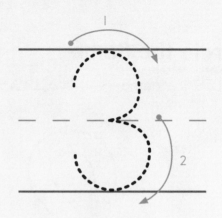

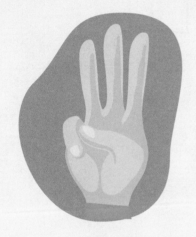

See It, Say It, Show It

This is the number **6**. SEE the number. SAY the number. SHOW the number using your fingers. TRACE the **6** with your finger.

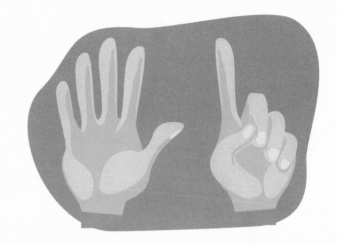

SIX

DRAW one ring on each of the six fingers.

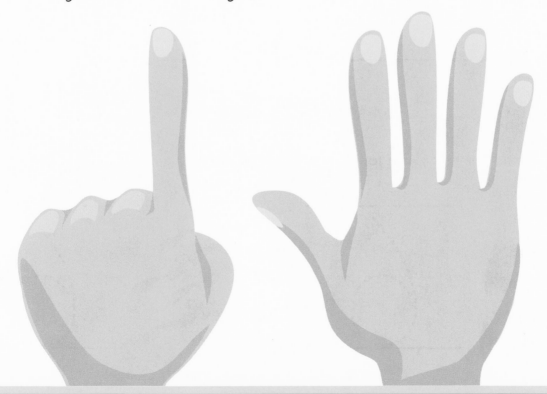

Number 6

Terrific Tracing

TRACE the number **6**s. Start at the green arrow labeled with a number 1.

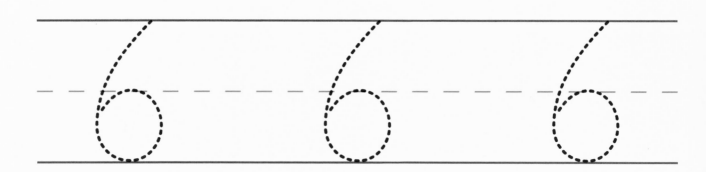

Now TRACE the number **6** next to each picture.

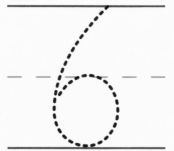

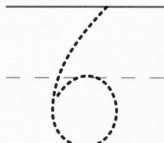

What's My Number?

COLOR the number 6. CIRCLE the pictures that show **six**.

Number 6

Color It

SHOW the number **six** using your fingers. COLOR the six ladybugs.

SHOW six fingers again. COLOR the six stars.

See It, Say It, Show It

This is the number **7**. SEE the number. SAY the number. SHOW the number using your fingers. TRACE the **7** with your finger.

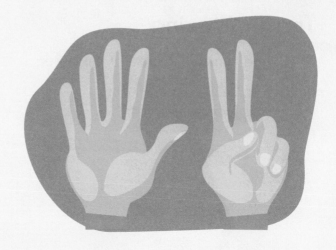

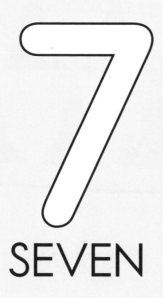

SEVEN

Here are seven ladybugs looking for seven flowers. DRAW seven flowers.

Terrific Tracing

TRACE the number **7**s. Start at the green arrow labeled with a number 1.

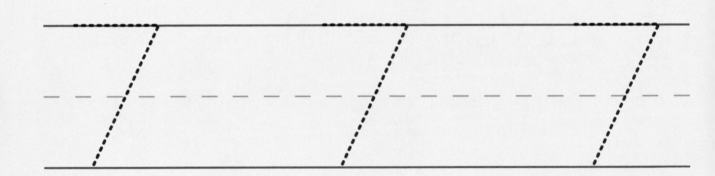

Now TRACE the number **7** next to each picture.

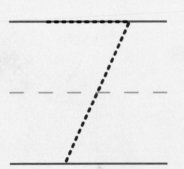

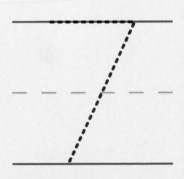

Hide and Seek

The secret **7**s are hiding from the pirates. FIND and CIRCLE the seven **7**s that are hiding in the picture.

Hop to It

DRAW a line connecting the **7**s to help the mother rabbit hop home to her seven babies.

See It, Say It, Show It

This is the number **8**. SEE the number. SAY the number. SHOW the number using your fingers. TRACE the **8** with your finger.

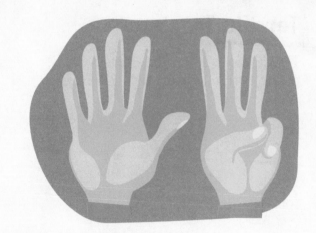

EIGHT

Here are eight snowmen. DRAW eight hats.

Terrific Tracing

TRACE the number 8s. Start at the green arrow labeled with a number 1.

legs

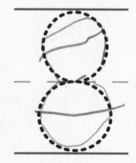
beetles

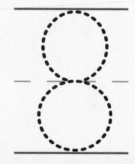
butterflies

Put It Away

DRAW lines to put away the groups of eight in the desk drawer.

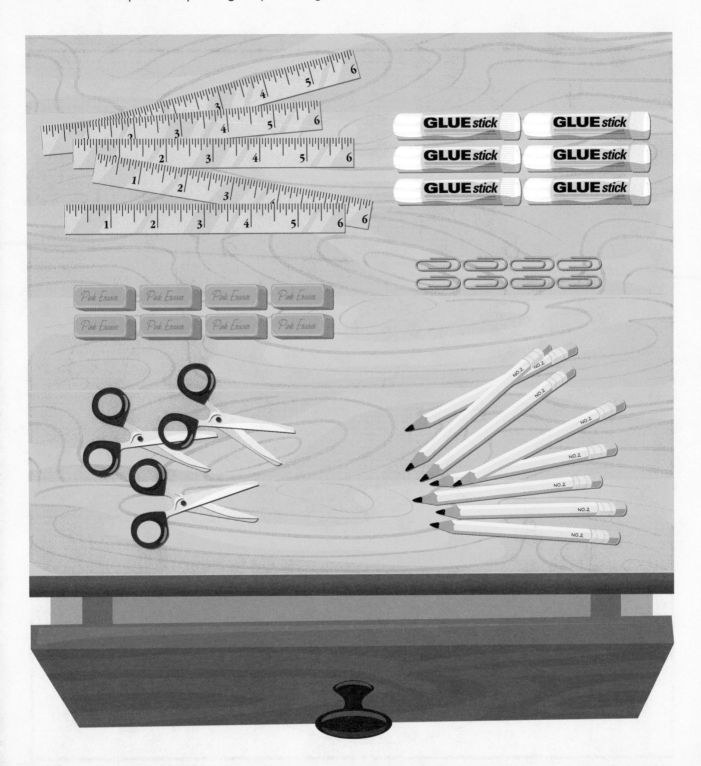

Color by Number

FIND the spaces with the number **8**. COLOR these spaces blue to see the picture.

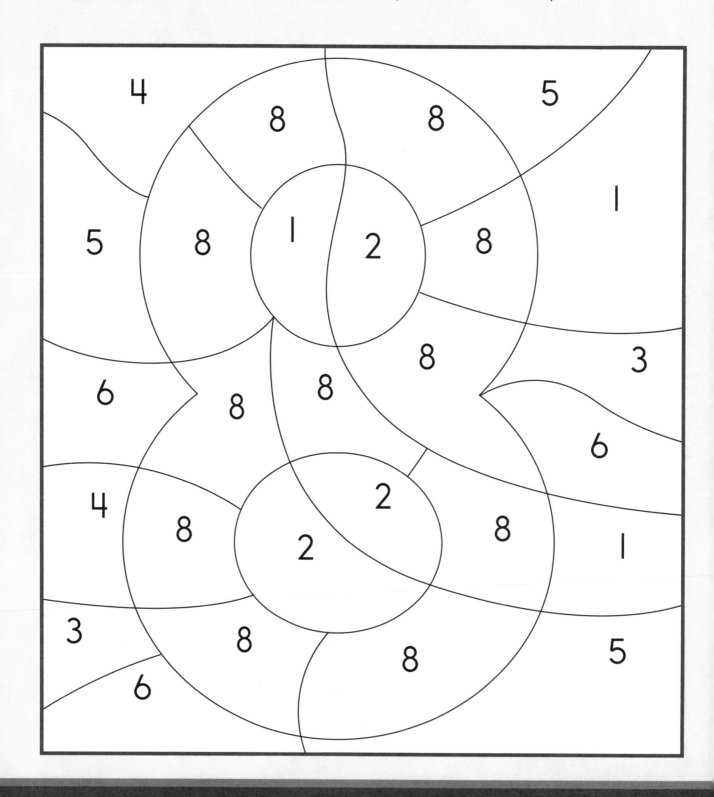

See It, Say It, Show It

This is the number **9**. SEE the number. SAY the number. SHOW the number using your fingers. TRACE the **9** with your finger.

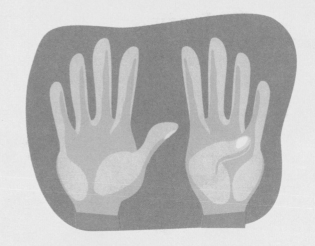

NINE

Here are nine presents. DRAW nine bows.

Terrific Tracing

TRACE the number **9**s. Start at the green arrow labeled with a number 1.

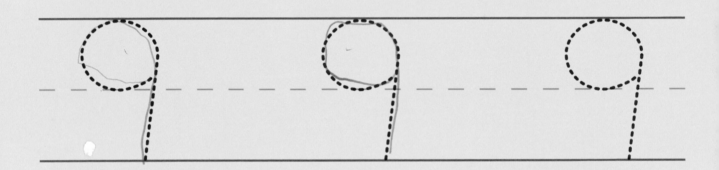

Now TRACE the number **9** next to each picture.

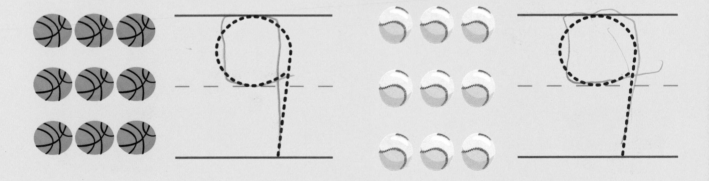

Draw It

There are nine players on the Nutty Nines team. COLOR the **9** on each of their shirts.

Maze Craze

DRAW a path through the **9**s to help the candle get to the birthday cake.

See It, Say It, Show It

This is the number 10. SEE the number. SAY the number. SHOW the number using your fingers. TRACE the 10 with your finger.

10
TEN

Here is a leopard. DRAW ten spots on the leopard.

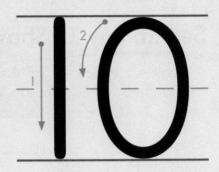

Terrific Tracing

TRACE the number 10s. Start at the green arrow labeled with a number 1.

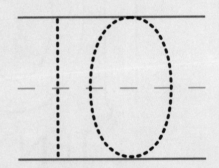

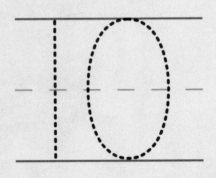

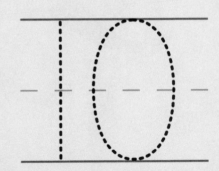

Color It

SHOW the number **ten** using your fingers. COLOR the ten baseballs.

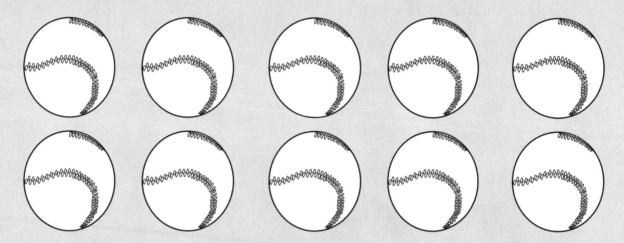

SHOW ten fingers again. COLOR the ten bats.

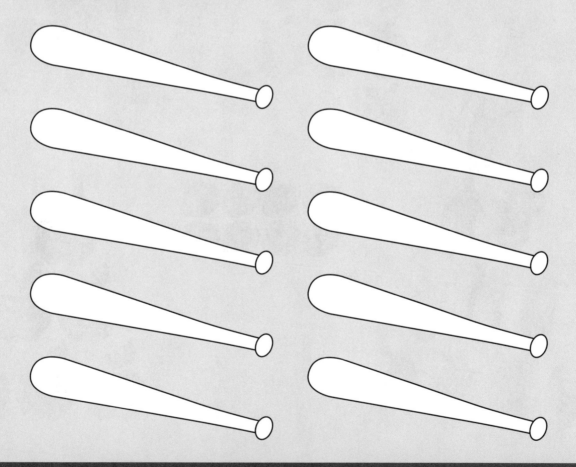

Number 10

What's Different?

TRACE the number 10. Then CROSS OUT the pictures that do **not** show **ten**.

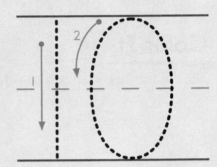

More than Enough

LOOK at the hands. In each row, CIRCLE the pair of hands that is holding up **more** fingers.

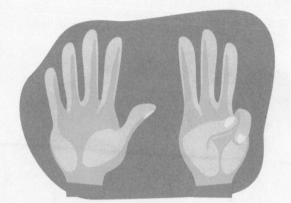 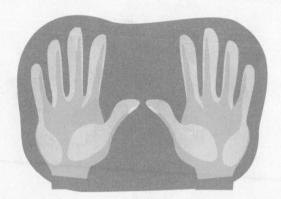

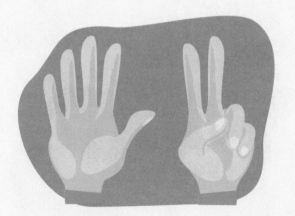 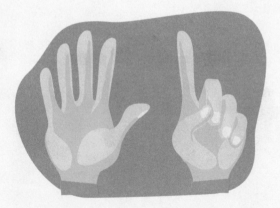

Don't Mess with Less

LOOK at the broccoli on each plate. CIRCLE the plate that has **less** broccoli on it.

Circle the Same

COLOR the numbers. Then CIRCLE the pictures that match the number at the top.

Put It Away

DRAW lines to put away the different groups of things in the recycling bins where they belong.

Color by Number

FOLLOW the directions to COLOR each part of the picture.

1 =  2 =  3 =   4 = 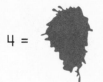 5 =

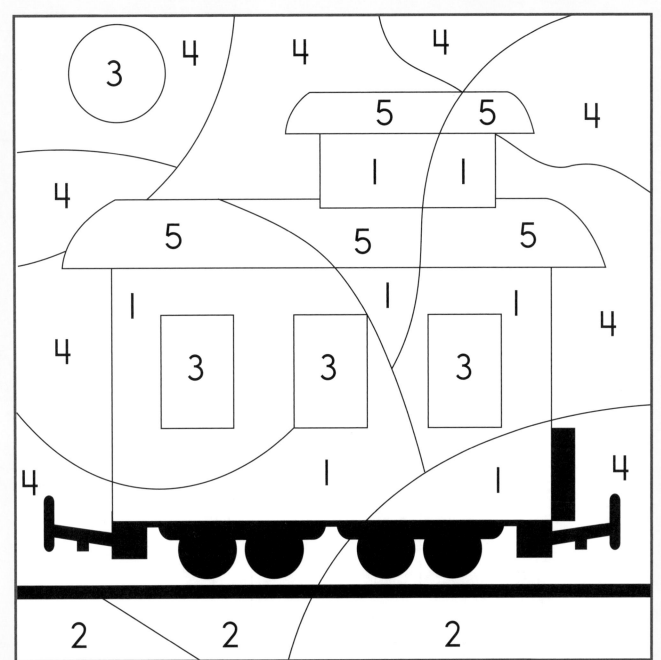

Color by Number

FOLLOW the directions to COLOR each part of the picture.

6 =    7 = 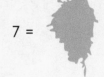   8 =   9 =    10 =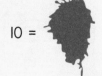

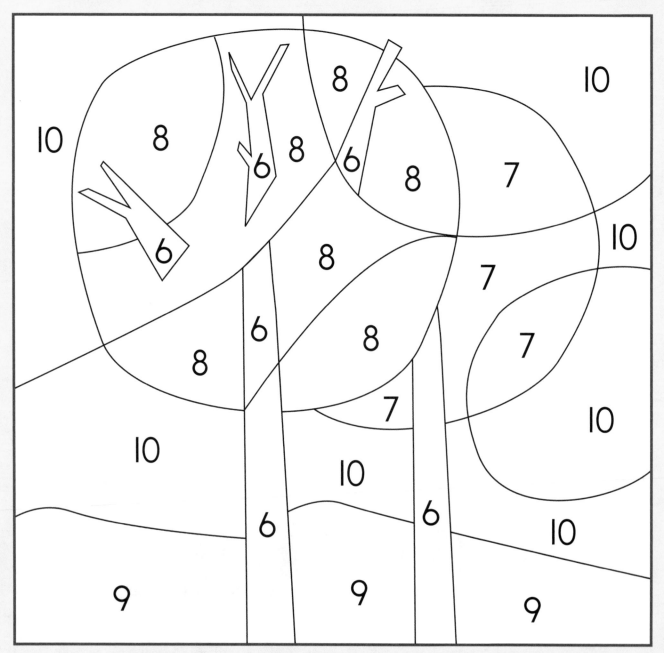

Hide and Seek

FIND and CIRCLE the numbers that are hiding in the picture.

Review

Match Up

TRACE the number on each box. DRAW a line from each group of crayons to the correct box.

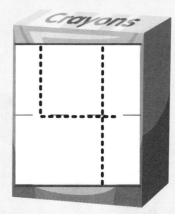

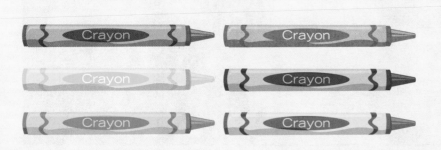
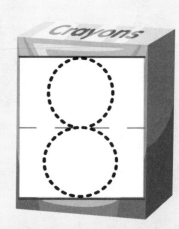

54

Super Sea Dive

LOOK at the picture. FIND and CIRCLE the numbers 1, 2, 3, 4, 5, 6, 7, 8, 9, and 10 in the water.

Terrific Tracing

TRACE the numbers on the sidewalk.

Page 3

Suggestion:

Page 5

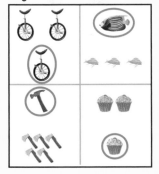

Page 6

Page 7

Suggestion:

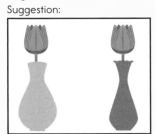

Page 9

Page 10

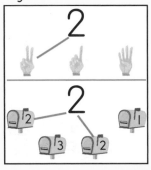

Page 11

Suggestion:

Page 13

Page 17

Page 18

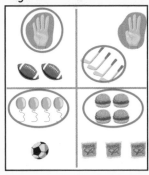

Page 19

Suggestion:

Page 21

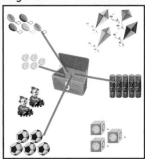

Page 22

Page 23

Page 24

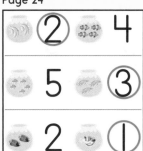

Answers

Page 25

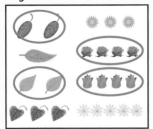

Page 26

Page 27

Suggestion:

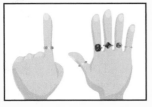

Page 29

Page 31

Suggestion:

Page 33

Page 34

Page 35

Suggestion:

Page 37

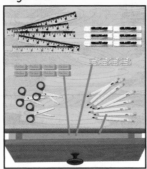

Page 38

Page 39

Suggestion:

Page 42

Page 43

Suggestion:

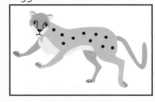

Page 46

Answers

Page 47

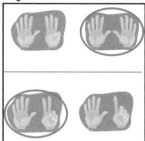

Page 48

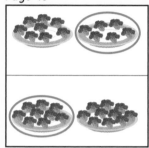

Page 49

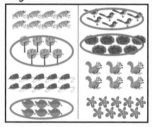

Page 50

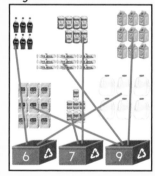

Page 51

Page 52

Page 53

Page 54

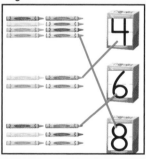

Page 55

Check out Sylvan's complete line of offerings!

SINGLE-SUBJECT WORKBOOKS

☑ Pre-K–5th grade

☑ Focus on individual skills and subjects

☑ Fun activities and exercises

3-IN-1 SUPER WORKBOOKS

☑ Pre-K–5th grade

☑ Three Sylvan single-subject workbooks in one package

☑ Perfect practice for the student who needs to focus on a range of topics

A $39 value for just $18.99!

FUN ON THE RUN ACTIVITY BOOKS

☑ Kindergarten–2nd grade

☑ Just $3.99/$4.75 Can.

☑ Colorful games and activities for on-the-go learning

FLASHCARD SETS

☑ Spelling for Kindergarten–2nd grade

☑ Vocabulary for 3rd–5th grade

☑ Includes 230 words to help students reinforce skills

PAGE PER DAY WORKBOOKS

☑ Pre-K–1st grade

☑ Perforated pages—perfect for your child to do just one workbook page each day

☑ Extra practice the easy way!

Try FREE pages today at SylvanPagePerDay.com

Sylvan Learning

With just a **PAGE PER DAY**, your child gets extra practice ... the easy way! Get sample pages for free!

Whether the goal is to get a jumpstart on new material or to brush up on past lessons, setting aside a small amount of time each day to complete one Sylvan workbook page will help your child review and improve skills, grow self-confidence, and develop a love of learning.

Visit SylvanPagePerDay.com to get free workbook printables in the grade of your choice!

CUT ALONG THE DOTTED LINE

Sylvan Learning